RETURN JOURNEY

The Friar's Bush Press
24 College Park Avenue
Belfast BT7 1LR
First Published 1987
Reprinted 1999
© Copyright reserved
ISBN 0946872 07 4

Printed by W&G Baird Ltd, Antrim, Northern Ireland

 Subsidised by the Arts Council of Northern Ireland (1987)

Return Journey

● BELFAST AND BEYOND ●

● PHOTOGRAPHS BY ARTHUR CAMPBELL ●

1 9 3 6 – 1 9 3 9

Foreword by Michael Longley

THE FRIAR'S BUSH PRESS

To my mother, Margretta Campbell
(Gretta Bowen, artist)
1880-1981
and my brothers Stanley and George

FOREWORD

IN HIS FIRST photograph the schoolgirl and the gentleman striding down the opposite pavement cross the path of the working man in his duncher. To the left and to the right they walk out of the picture and begin to age, and then to die. But the pain they cause us is made exquisite by their continuing presences close to the elderly woman who hesitates on the kerb, and the newspaper seller who stands his ground and advertises a headline that was out of date years ago.

Like all the people pictured in Arthur Campbell's folio, these characters disturb our sense of past and present because our present is now their future, whether they are alive or dead. What is near changes places with what is distant. Time and space are confused. And always the magical transformations depend on detail: Ford Populars, turn-ups on trousers, deep hat-bands, tin advertisements for Caffrey's Stout, gas lamps, trams: the hustle and bustle generated by so many folk fifty years ago — or, as in one of the photographs of the Balmoral Show, at 3.12 p.m. precisely on 27th May 1938. We listen across the decades for the King's Hall clock ticking off the seconds.

These photographs were taken during the three years before I was born. I have found it impossible not to search for familiar faces. In every instance my parents are waiting in the wings or have wandered out of focus. But the roofs forming a backdrop to the tractor on page 44 belong to houses in Harberton Park which leads to the street where I grew up. Other pictures bring back to me with a heart-stopping shock, horse troughs, shawlies, carrier bikes, drinking fountains. Out of the corner of my eye I catch myself or my twin brother swaying down the spiral staircase above the tramdriver's white hat on page 3. Our Sunday walk took us down the now widened and spoiled road to Shaw's Bridge and the Minnowburn, both lovingly recorded by Campbell, the ford V8 parked in one picture as fleeting a presence as the swan that glides across the other.

Before writing this preface I visited an exhibition in the Ulster Museum of the photographs of A. R. Hogg, one of Arthur Campbell's great predecessors. The urchins in Hogg's pictures go barefoot: those in Campbell's wear shoes. There must have been other improvements in the thirty years since 1907, but somehow the general deportment of the people in Hogg's photographs displays a style and vitality which seems to be absent here. Looking at a group of Hogg's dandy young shop assistants, one wonders how many survived the Somme. How many survivors from the Trenches appear in Campbell's photographs? The expressions on the faces in these pages suggest that they know only too well that they have not inherited a land fit for heroes. There is often something drab, anaemic, disappointed, apprehensive about them. The Thirties were of course a time of economic depression and unemployment, as some of Campbell's pictures show. The photograph on page 26 of the premature sandbags being taken from grounds of the City Hall in 1937 also reminds us of the menace hanging in the air with the smoke and fine cinder from the mill chimneys. Four years later the Luftwaffe were to top drop tons of bombs on a shamefully unprepared city.

Belfast has been changed as much by planners and developers as by the bombs of the Luftwaffe or, thirty years later, the IRA. At a time of accelerated and confusing change both in the city and the countryside, Arthur Campbell the rememberer is an important citizen. He has emerged belatedly from the shadow of his brother George and his mother Gretta Bowen, as a true artist in his own right, curious and sensitive and alert to everything around him except the value of his work. With his camera, his box of tricks, he shows us that seeing what's there and recording it honestly are the only tricks that matter. It is a privilege to accompany him on his reconnaissance of our past.

Michael Longley   *15 June 1987*

Arthur Campbell photographed at Larne railway station by James G. McCay, 7 July 1935

INTRODUCTION

THIS RETROSPECTIVE of the Thirties in Belfast and beyond, is the outcome of my buying a camera in 1936. It was tiny and noiseless and made 1$\frac{1}{2}$ x 1$\frac{1}{4}$ inch negatives. It went with me in the city and was joined by a sketch book and pencil on country jaunts.

It has been said that photographers have an unresolvable quandary between recording and shaping. The problem is common to all makers of images; learnt early by artists and those who look through a viewfinder and my work has been picture-making by camera, brush, pen and words. I am not an antiquary or historian, except incidentally or accidentally when I happen upon something that takes my fancy.

The landscape painter does his shaping by moving a tree or omitting it. A photographer may accept what is in front of him and be a reporter, or shape his picture by composing it after careful study. An alternative is to go away and come back when a change of light or season makes the subject matter acceptable. When, however, I saw something interesting, I knew that I might not see it again. Delay or ask for more sun and the moment could pass, so I was alert to the boys with their delivery bikes, the driver of the Causeway tram, the transient snow scene and the ash coming into bud in April. Many photographs had to be 'shot from the hip' because it was snap or go without. Others were the result of much circling and cogitation, always in the knowledge that there were limits to the patience of my companions.

If my pictures have any significance now, they have acquired it by the passage of fifty years. I certainly never had in mind anything but the making of a personal archive and a pictorial chronicle of the passing show. As a 'snapper up of unconsidered trifles', I unwittingly recorded some social history. It did not occur to me in my days as a novice that I might be photographing for generations to come and it is my regret that the forlorn furniture, antiques, Victoriana and stalls of second-hand books in Smithfield market were not matter for my lens. The market was assumed to be a fixture like the tramcars, street lavatories and the gate lodge at Botanic gardens, which were taken for granted yet disappeared virtually overnight.

I liked to record places that I found for myself, or to search for new slants on well known ones. I am interested in townscape although hard put to say why. The design made by some streets appeals to me: their design and character. I found material for photography and painting in places like Mount Charles (before its upper end was turned into a car park) and the Crescent in Belfast, and in Dublin, Manchester and London. The tactile nature of stone and the texture of worn brick and granite intrigue me.

The Holiday Fellowship walking group, still flourishing, took me into the countryside on Saturdays and from it sprang the youth hostel movement in 1931. Members were offered a return fare from Belfast to Newcastle for about half-a crown and a night in a bunk in a Mournes hostel cost one shilling, I got to know the mountains well.

Excursion party—W. & G. Baird Ltd and *Belfast Telegraph*
employees outside their offices where Library Street joins
Royal Avenue, 7 July 1929. Arthur Campbell worked here as
a printing designer 1925-45. *(Belfast Telegraph)*

Ireland's Saturday Night paid four shillings when I reported a rugby match, (two shillings when it rained off), which helped with sallies to the Antrim coast. The *Belfast Telegraph* published a Mournes photograph taken with a friend's camera; then another, and another . . . and continues to print an occasional one. I also wrote from the mid-thirties for the photographic journals, some magazines, and modest fees helped to pay for film and prints.

The Thirties were anything but 'good old days'. In my school days, destitute men and women sat along the kerb on the Lisburn Road at night, waiting for the Union Gate to open, then tossed their bottles into the gutter and surged inside for the obligatory bath before bed. Woolworths displayed large cans of Brasso at sixpence and the down-and-outs drank the methylated spirit that stayed on top of the sediment. An alternative to blunt the sharp edge of their misery was 'toney wine'.

Tuberculosis and unemployment were the scourges of these and subsequent years. Enlightened treatment, diet, hygiene, housing and sanitation vanquished the 'White Death', for it was for long a mass killer. There were wars in the mid-thirties in Abyssinia and Spain and some of us hauled a handcart to collect food and medicines for Spain. The big war did not come until the end of the decade and, ironically, it raised our living standards. Tuberculosis, the Union Workhouse (now long submerged in the City Hospital), 'paupers' brown' clothes, the Poor Law, linen mills, pawn shops, coal, gas and archaic dispensaries are unlamented memories held by old people. Nobody hungers in the Welfare State, or goes without treatment because he cannot pay a doctor. There is still a lack of jobs.

The fear of war in 1937, made me call off a climbing holiday in the Ardennes. Local defence forces (forerunners of the Home Guard) were formed and barricades erected. When the threat passed the sandbags were taken out of the City Hall grounds. It will be seen in the photograph that Richardson Sons and Owden's building (not yet become the Water Office, or later, Marks and Spencer), had a high-pitched roof, which was destroyed by incendiary bombs in the 1941 air raids.

A flower-woman would be trampled under foot in today's Donegall Place, and the Fiat 'Mickey Mouse' car is now a thing of the past. The Grand Central Hotel has been demolished in the recent vast clearance. Trams could be seen passing the hotel and the recent sharp eyed may catch a glimpse of the kiosk at Castle Junction which was laughingly known as the 'trammymen's dance hall'. The turn-ups on trousers and the deep hatbands belong to the age, every bit as much as the lamp and tram standards.

Most authors of books of nostalgic content have to dig their material out of files. I have lived long enough to compile my own commentary. This book is restricted to the Thirties, so I am left free to select from what I have for subsequent years and perhaps make another book. May this one give some pleasure.

Arthur Campell 11 May 1987

This is the view from the hallway of No 10 Royal Avenue, where the Northern Ireland Road Transport Board had set up offices following its absorption of independent bus companies. I was seconded from the *Belfast Telegraph* to advise the Board on publicity and visited the offices on most days . . . usually armed with my camera.

The Royal Avenue Hotel was next to Thomas Cook's and the floors above the travel agency were part of the hotel. Where better to start a 'Cook's Tour' of Belfast and beyond.

18 October 1937

When commercial travellers came from Britain, they entrusted their cumbersome cases of samples to a corps of handcart men who attended the cross-channel steamers, produced the cases at interviews, and placed them in hotel stock rooms. This man is taking a breather before crossing Royal Avenue to the Grand Central Hotel which is seen on the righthand edge of the photograph.

18 July 1937

White linen covers for the caps of tram
conductors and drivers were issued on
the first day of each summer.
18 July 1936

Gresham Street, has long been the home of pet shops and was once described as the city's 'pocket zoo'. The side of the street which was festooned with cages, will disappear under the redevelopment plans announced recently.

2 November 1936

The *Belfast Telegraph* newspaper stabled its horses and delivery vans in Gordon street and had a large store around the corner in Library Street for its huge reels of newsprint paper. One child offered me a bite of her 'piece' while I took the photograph.

20 August 1936

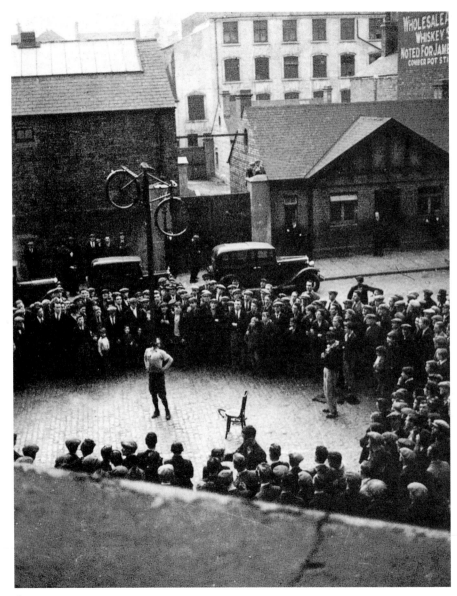

Street 'turns' earned much appreciated pennies in the harsh Thirties. Here, a bicycle is balanced on top of a pole resting on a man's chin. Another busker, flowers around his neck, strums a banjo and (on this side of the chair) a third collects the coppers in his cap.

22 September 1936

A royal visit to Belfast meant gaily decked streets and buildings and much ceremonial marching by troops. It will be seen that ranks of four had not yet given way to three and puttees were still worn: the strips of the khaki cloth wound spirally round the leg from ankle to knee as a kind of gaiters.

28 July 1937

Royal Avenue at the Central Library, 1937. The snow was easing but collars were still turned up and a shawl gave warmth.

12 March 1937

Taken through a ground floor window of the *Belfast
Telegraph* with snow still falling and becoming slush churned
by soaked feet.

12 March 1937

These boys met in Alexandra Park while on their rounds. Parkside Gardens is in the background. There was time for a quick chat; then on with their deliveries.

Sam Cochrane was the big name in bikes. He sold BSA carrier bikes in Gresham Street and Shaftesbury Square in Belfast and at Lisburn and Lurgan; price £7 each or on easy terms of thirteen shillings (65p) a month or four shillings (20p) a week. An ordinary pushbike cost much less.

28 September 1936

There were street fountains in Belfast; some, like this one, for pedestrians and large ones for cattles and horses on their way to or from the steamers or a lairage. This fountain was on the Antrim Road a short distance from Carlisle Circus.

15 Septemer 1936

The 'grand floral staircase' was the spine
of Bellevue pleasure gardens which were
opened in 1920. It carried visitors from
Antrim Road to the plateau under the
cliffs of Cave Hill. The zoological
collection was laid out on either side of
the staircase and was officially opened
by the Lord Mayor, Sir Crawford
McCullagh, Bart., on 28 March 1934.

1936

The Plateau at Bellevue tailed off at its northern (Whitewell)
end with a boating pool, a merry-go-round, slot machines
and an amusement fair.

13 August 1937

Masts towering above the sheds took me to York Dock in 1936 and from it I looked across to the windjammer 'Lawhill' waiting for ballast in Spencer Basin. She was a four-masted barque high in the water after unloading a cargo of Australian wheat.

The exciting grain races by sailing ships were nearing their end that year, as steam took over, and the 'Lawhill' was one of the last tall ships to come to Belfast.

She was built in 1892 at Dundee and, much later, was bought by Captain Gostav Eriksen of Finland. She was broken up around 1958.

Unloading slates and tiles from a sailing
coaster in Clarendon Dock, Belfast
harbour.

25 August 1936

York Dock, 1936. Unloading a cargo, in this case maize, was hard manual work and risky at times. It was not unknown for a load to slip out of its slings.

25 August 1936

The tide is out at Queen's Bridge Quay,
known colloquially as the Sand Quay.
Below the chimneys of the electricity
power station is the iron railway bridge
which sometimes carried excursion
trains to the County Down line.

9 June 1938

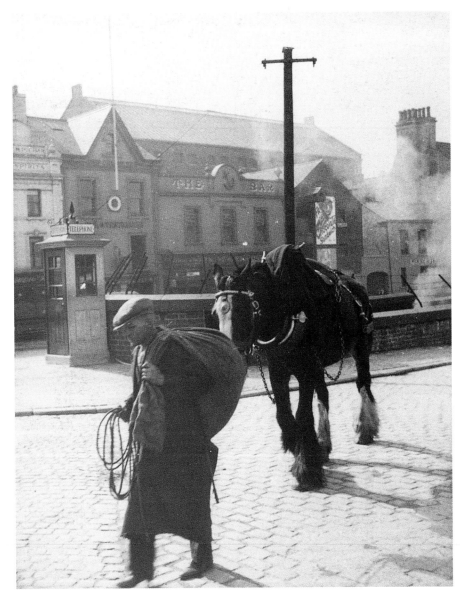

The trace of smoke seen on the righthand edge was coming from a goods train steaming from Donegall Quay, at Queen's Bridge and about to go underground. The telephone kiosk is directly over the short tunnel that had its outlet on the far side of the bridge. Ship chandlers James Tedford & Sons, (see the mast and lifebelt), are still much alive but the Anchor Bar is no more.

9 June 1938

Almost all loads were transported by
horse-drawn lorries and vans, so
drinking troughs were placed
strategically. This photograph was taken
at the point where Laganbank Road
joined Oxford Street beside Queen's
Bridge. The automobile showroom was
Agnew & Graham's.

17 September 1936

These newsvendors were stationed beside Sawer's in High Street close to Lombard Street, 1937. The *Irish Press* was a comparative newcomer to publishing. I have not seen the Scottish newspaper *The Bulletin* for a long time but it was popular in the Thirties in Belfast.

10 March 1937

The Fiat Topolino (or 'Mickey Mouse') was introduced in 1936 and went on to sell more than half a million. A flower woman and basket would get short shrift in today's Donegall Place. Just visible beside the Bank Buildings (on left), now Primark, was the Provincial Bank which is today part of Allied Irish Banks. Beyond, in Royal Avenue, is the tower of the Grand Central, an hotel which disappeared in a recent widescale clearance. In the foreground a man is peering into the window of William Mullan & Son Ltd., a bookshop still going strong, and immediately behind him is a glimpse of the tramways information kiosk which was laughingly called the "Trammymen's dance hall." Even the turn-ups on trousers and the deep hat-bands are pointers to the time, as are the tram and lamp standards.

20 November 1936

Cars from overseas were a rarity in 1937. This one is from California. Trams caused congestion in Donegall Place which was not helped by the absence of parking restrictions.

25 June 1937

The City Hall was the backdrop to this corner of Wellington Place at the Scottish Provident Buildings.

28 August 1936

The Ford Popular was the first motor car to be sold for not more than £100. A man can be seen working on top of one of the City Hall's flood lights.

9 July 1937

Imperial House was a recent addition to
Donegall Square East. It is seen here
through the *porte-cochere* of the City
Hall. The Union Flag and decorations
celebrate the Coronation of George VI.

11 May 1937

Donegall Square North. In 1937 there was a threat of war and precautions were taken; here the sandbags are being taken out of the City Hall grounds when the war scare passed.
Robinson & Cleaver's is on the left and just past it is Richardson Sons & Owden's, later to become the Water Office and now Marks & Spencer's. It had a high pitched roof which was lost to incendiary bombs in the 1941 air raids. The Titantic memorial can be seen as a white statue in the roadway between the sandbags and the truck.

6 October 1938

26

Flower sellers have long been a feature of the railings at the front of the city Hall. The Queen Victoria Statue is seen through the foliage and in the distance is Donegall Square Methodist church.

3 October 1937

A revolution began in the roof space of this motor car showroom in Donegall Square East. There, Harry Ferguson did the experimental work which took mechanised farming a giant step ahead. It is reckoned that 85 of every 100 tractors of all makes are built on his principles. Immediately above the last window on the right protruded the steel beam used to lift machinery that could not negotiate the stairs. It was removed when the building became a bank.

3 October 1937

Harry Ferguson (Motors) Ltd, founded in 1911, was the Austin distributor for Northern Ireland and was also renowned for the quality of its used cars and vans. This photograph is of its secondhand car showrooms in Alfred Street.

4 August 1937

Today's Queen Mother was queen and George VI was king
when this street artist was chalking at the City Hall railings in
1937.

8 July 1937

Belfast was *en fete* for the visit of
George VI and Queen Elizabeth —
today's Queen' Mother — and crash
barriers kept Donegall Place clear for
the royal entourage.

27 July 1937

Dolce far niente! There was no one-way or restricted-entry
around the City Hall in June 1937. Fifty years have brought
many changes to the part of Wellington Place seen here.

3 June 1937

32

William Mullan & Son Ltd, the long-established booksellers of Donegall Place, had a children's shop in Fountain Street.

20 July 1937

A view of the City Hall from Donegall
Square West. The bunting and garlands
are in honour of the royal visitors.
27 July 1937

The number plate of this Morris 12
visitor from Egypt demonstrates how our
numerical system is derived from Arabic
figures. The car is parked where
Donegall Square West and Howard Street
meet.

3 September 1936

Hugh Greer's second-hand book shop
and stalls were at the corner of Queen
Street and Wellington Street. He had
another shop in Gresham Street.

8 March 1937

City donkeys were survivals from poorer days and already disappearing from Belfast. This one, with bales of scrap cloth, was coming along Howard Street to edge into the traffic at the City Hall. Its bridle grasped, the man trudged beside the donkey, throwing it or his helper on the footpath an occasional word.

23 September 1936

The crew of this Belfast Corporation tower wagon is curing a hiccup in the tramway's overhead wires where Cromac Street and Ormeau Avenue meet. (The tall standard was one of 15,000 gas lamps in Belfast.)

2 November 1936

Coke, a by-product of the coal in the gasworks, was cheap and much-prized as fuel in 1936 by those who lived in the Cromac Street district. The boys said they paid two pence for a sackful.

3 September 1936

Facing the main gate of the Botanic Gardens on University Road in 1937 were Dundee's, chemists, Post Office, and Rigby & Milner's, confectioners. The site is now occupied by the Ulster Bank and a new Post Office. This was probably the last barrel organ in Belfast.

11 February 1937

School was out. A pupil had crossed the road from methodist College and was waiting for a Malone Road tram. The building with a clock tower was the lodge at the entrance to the Botanic Gardens.

15 March 1937

This is the rear of King's Hall in the Royal Ulster Agricultural Society's showgrounds at Balmoral, Belfast. The Society was founded in 1826. The 30-acres are an animated scene every May when Balmoral Show takes place: the largest single display of animals and machinery in Northern Ireland, with horse-jumping and other attractions.

27 May 1938

Harry Ferguson's bankers refused him financial support when he wanted to start a farm machinery manufacturing business. "Your project isn't feasible, Mr. Ferguson. Tractors will never take the place of horses on farms or in the city". His Coventry factory, which he eventually sold to Massey-Ferguson, sold a record five million tractors — Fergusons and Massey-Fergusons — up to the end of 1984 for a turnover of £1.7 billion. Seen here is the first Ferguson tractor to be shown in Northern Ireland, at Balmoral Show, 1937.

27 May 1937

Harry Ferguson used a ten-year-old boy and the boy's father to drive and put across the safety and simplicity of his system in a demonstration at Balmoral, May 1938. The tractor is one of his earliest ones and was made for him by David Brown's of Huddersfield, Yorkshire.

25 May 1938

Ploughing at Gilnahirk on the outskirts of east Belfast.
2 May 1936

Carrying hay up the slope from Shaw's
Bridge to Malone Road.

28 August 1936

The well-known beeches along the road
that leads to Ballylesson and on to
Lisburn. The gateposts mark the
beginning of the secondary road to
Edenderry and the stream is the
Minnowburn, a tributary of the River
Lagan. The car was the recently
introduced Ford V8.

3 May 1936

Shaw's Bridge and the River Lagan,
south Belfast.

28 August 1936

The Minnowburn, south Belfast, in winter.

15 March 1937

Riders in the 1938 Ulster Grand Prix coming off the Seven-
Mile-Straight to round Clady Corner on their way to the fast
stretch past the grand stand.

20 August 1938

Chris Tattersall was adjusting the
carburettor of his CTS home-built
machine at Thorn Cottage in the 1936
Ulster Grand Prix which was run over
the Clady circuit. A hole in the hedge
gave a good view and one could always
draw the head in when a policeman or
race marshall was doing his rounds.

22 August 1936

Walter Rusk was out of luck in the 1937 Ulster Grand Prix motor cycle race over the old Clady circuit. He was the first rider to lap the course at more than one hundred miles an hour but died the following year.

19 August 1937

Acclamation from the pits for Stanley Woods, seen finishing
to win the 350cc class race at the 1939 Ulster Grand Prix.
19 August 1939

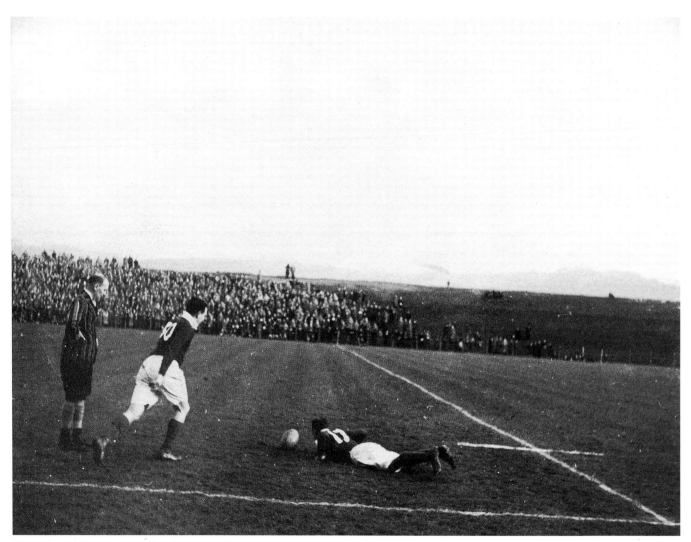

The Lions — the Rugby Union tourists to South Africa —
played Hartley's Selected XV at Ravenhill, Belfast. Here G. J.
Morgan is placing the ball for V. G. J. Jenkins, who
converted the try.   April 1939

Faces in the crowd at the Schools Cup
Final at Ravenhill on Saint Patrick's Day,
1938.

17 March 1938

A London Midland & Scottish tender locomotive in York Road station.

25 August 1936

▶

Newcastle station was the terminus of two railway routes from Belfast: the Great Northern and the Belfast and County Down. The G.N.R. trains meandered through a large part of the countryside and took in Ballyroney and Castlewellan, and it was alleged that if one got a shave before leaving, another was needed in Newcastle. A libel on the County Down's speed was "Ye can pick flowers out of the windas; aye, an' watch them coming into bloom", but good time was made to Newcastle in the short six-wheeled carriages which the system retained until its dying day.

26 September 1936

The railway that once joined Ballymoney (on the main Belfast Londonderry line) to Ballycastle on the north Antrim coast, was owned by the Northern Counties Committee of the London Midland and Scottish. It operated on a narrow gauge of three feet and transporter trucks with the standard 5 foot 3 inch carried the little engines when they moved to the main line. The photograph is of a compound 2-4-2 tank locomotive in Ballycastle station. (One locomotive earned itself a place in railway history in 1943 by running past the platform, through a wall, and on to the road outside the station!)

16 April 1938

The Thirties were hard times for farmers as for everyone, so do-it-yourself ruled and this gate of plaited branches was typical. The photograph was taken in 1938, at Raholp, near Downpatrick, where Saint Patrick landed in 432 AD.

3 July 1938

The 'Causeway Tram' near Portballintrae on its way to Portrush from the Giant's Causeway. The Rev. Jonathan Simpson, Presbyterian minister in Portrush objected to the tram running on Sundays and was inveighing against it when the tram rattled loudly while going round a sharp curve nearby. "There You are, Lord, You can hear it for Yourself", he shouted. It is alleged that at a harvest service he said "We thank thee, Lord, for this bountiful harvest. All is gathered safely except for a wheen of stooks at Ballywillan and it is their fault, for they are lazy, Lord".

17 September 1938

The 'Causeway Tram' made its way the nine miles from Portrush to Dunluce Castle, Bushmills, and the Giant's Causeway, in parts along the edge of the cliffs. The tramway was the first passenger system in the world to generate electricity from water. It was officially opened in 1883 by Lord Spencer — greatgrandfather of Diana Princess of Wales — who was Lord Lieutenant of Ireland, and closed after sixty-six years.

17 September 1938

A Leyland Tiger bus waiting at Larne station to take train
passengers along the Antrim Coast to its destination at
Cushendun. N.B. 'Cushendum'!

16 July 1938

The Belfast and County Down Railway branched off from the main line to serve Newtownards and Donaghadee. This bus of the Northern Ireland Road Transport Board stands outside Donaghadee railway station, loading for the journey down the Ards Peninsula.

24 July 1937

Torr Head, in the north-east of County Antrim, is the nearest point in Ireland to mainland Britain. The photograph shows the signal station operated by Lloyd's to monitor shipping in the dangerous 'Waters of Moyle'. The Mull of Kintyre is on the horizon fifteen miles distant.

16 August 1939

On an Easter visit to Torr Head signal station on the north Antrim Coast, we were shown the lockers full of the flags that were used to semaphore to passing ships. The seamen danced hornpipes and we returned the compliment with jigs and reels while David Elliott supplied flute music.

19 April, Easter 1938

Chimney Rock Mountain (2,152 feet) is a popular and easy climb in the Mourne Mountains, not far from Newcastle. Slieve Donard (2,796 feet and the highest mountain in Northern Ireland) is on the right; it is separated from

Chimney Rock by a valley and the Bloody Bridge River.
24 September 1939

The scene was Green Harbour between Newcastle and Annalong, County Down, and the blankets were being folded in front of a Holiday Fellowship cottage. The youth hostel movement in Northern Ireland grew out of that walking-cum-social group in 1931.

Members were expected to do all chores: cook (and wash up); make their beds; leave not a scrap of litter; and respect the countryside. Their aim was to "Leave nothing behind but a good impression".

The Ulster Society for the Preservation of the Countryside had its origin in H.F. and the Y.H. Association.

27 June 1937

Much enthusiasm went into the appeal for contributions to buy Whitepark Bay in north Antrim in order to extinguish the toll that was charged to get to the beach. The Youth Hostel Association joined Holiday Fellowship and conservation minded sympathisers and success came in 1938. Here Elsie Hamilton, with "OURS 1938" in pebbles marks the handing over of the bay to the National Trust for the use of the public. The appeal raised the agreed £1,250.

8 September 1938

The quarry overlooking Newcastle
harbour and Dundrum Bay, County
Down.

1 July 1939

The walkers and cyclists of Northern Ireland gave much voluntary help towards renovating and maintaining the houses where they stayed overnight. Here Walter Henry and James McCay are working at Ballagh cottage, which had started as a youth hostel and was taken over by Holiday Fellowship when the nearby Bloody Bridge hostel was opened.

24 November 1935

The Glenveagh estate in County Donegal was strictly private in 1936 but we wheedled our way in and even walked timorously through the grounds of Glenveagh Castle without meeting a sinner. Some of the famous herd of red deer showed up on the mountainside across Lough Veagh.

10 June 1936

Brigid McClafferty had four of us as her first guests in her Poisoned Glen House in Dunlewey, County Donegal, 1938. Her brother John was our chauffeur on jaunts in Gweedore and as far as Bunbeg. Brigid is at the window.

7 September 1938

On Luke's Mountain in the Mournes.

10 July 1937